I0414988

A
CHASSIS
ALIGNMENT
PROCEDURE

FOR FORMULA CARS

October 1977
Reprint February 1995
Reprint January 1998
Reprint April 2010

Michael W. Velten
Delaware, Ohio 43015
stick@velten.net
USA

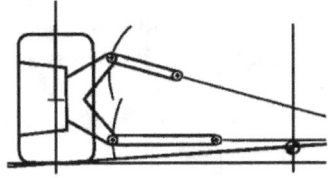

COPYRIGHT 1977-2010

All rights reserved. No part of this material may be reproduced in any form without permission in writing from the author.
ISBN 1451559283
EAN-13 is 9781451559286

ACKNOWLEDGMENTS

The content of this publication is derived from many years of actual hands-on experience driving, and aligning racing chassis. For their physical and moral support in this effort over these years I wish to thank my mother and father most of all. Without them it would not have been done.

I would also like to thank all of the many friends who have assisted throughout the years.

AUTHOR'S 2010 NOTE

It has been over thirty years since this book was originally published and technology has entered the racing world with tremendous impact. There are numerous tools available for measuring the alignment of your race car. While you can opt to use high tech tools, all of the principles in this book still hold true today. I would invite you to send me your thoughts on this book and your experiences with chassis alignment.

TABLE OF CONTENTS

I. INTRODUCTION

It is not the intended purpose of this document to specify the suspension settings or modifications that should be used for any given car, driver, or track condition. The purpose is rather to provide an accurate method of determining and altering the suspension settings of your race car.

There are many good sources of information available describing the theoretical consequences of changing roll centers, wheel camber, toe in, ride height, spring rates, roll stiffness etc.. If all of this theory were accurate, predictable, and well correlated to the real world, there would be only one right way to build a car for a given purpose (class). In our case, the purpose is to complete a given distance, over a given course in a shorter elapsed time than anyone else on the same course.

Since it is usually the opinion of the driver as to how a race car is operating, it is probably also the obligation of the driver to be aware of as much of the theory of suspension settings and chassis design as possible. To this end, I have suggested several good references covering the subject.

Whether the theory is understood and the adjustment is made in the correct direction is of little importance if the amount of the change is not known relative to some starting point. Even the actual numerical value of a suspension setting is of secondary importance to the ability to accurately measure the change in its value and note its effect on performance.

If your system of suspension checking and adjustment is repeatable, and adequate notes are kept on performance then predictions can be made with reasonable accuracy. The only advantage in using absolute numbers is in verbally comparing your findings to other drivers in similar cars. Here again, a driver's preference as to the handling characteristics of his car can often confuse a verbal discussion on the subject.

The following sections describe a complete and accurate method of measuring suspension setting on a formula car. The techniques described should be easily adaptable to other types of vehicles. The equipment described can, for the most part, be hand made and should be of minimal cost. There are perhaps tools available that would make the job slightly quicker but, I doubt, any more accurate.

II. TOOLS

Following is a description of the type of equipment needed to perform an accurate suspension alignment. The exact pieces must be tailored to the design and dimensions of your car, (e.g. strings and trammel bars must clear exhaust systems, wings, and other protrusions from the vehicle).

LEVEL SURFACE

An adequately level surface is perhaps the most difficult item to find and also the most important. A surface that is perfectly flat and large enough to contain the entire car with several feet of level area around it should be located. Shims are at best a compromise and make it difficult to measure ride height and the like. An acceptable compromise is perhaps to have a perfectly level surface, left to right, with a slight slope front to rear. If none of the above methods apply to your garage, then a set of leveling ramps can and should be made.

The ramps can be cut from good quality 2 x 10 inch planks. The resulting 1&1/2 x 8 inch boards can be laid one under both front wheels and one under both rear wheels (see figure 1). The planks should then be shimmed until level and the shims can then be nailed or glued in place. The planks should extend outboard of the wheels and tires at each end by about one foot. This system will then provide an accurate reference point from which to measure ride height and hub height. The planks should be painted to minimize warpage and their place on the floor marked. The planks should be placed on the floor separated by a distance that will allow ride height blocks to be placed between the planks and frame. Such positioning must also allow the car to sit on the planks with all four wheels and tires mounted.

PARALLEL STRING SUPPORTS

Two equal lengths of extruded aluminum with either a "T" or "I" cross section (nominally a 1 inch square cross section) will be used, one across the front and one across the rear at approximately hub height. See figures 1 and 4.

The bars should extend about 1 inch outboard of the widest part of the car (at hub height this is usually the tire side walls). The bars should be securely clamped together and a 1/16 inch hole drilled through both a half inch from each end. It is very important that these holes be exactly the same distance apart on both bars.

Next a support must be fabricated, front and rear, to hold the bars at approximately hub height in front of the front tires and to the rear of the rear tires. At the rear, a plate bolted to the gearbox and slotted for adjustment will normally support the rear bar at about the right height. At the front, the frame can often be used and occasionally spacers will be required to hold the bar in front of the tires. The purpose of these supports is not to provide an accurate jigging fixture but rather to firmly hold the crossbars with provision for adjustment left, right and vertically.

An alternate method of supporting the bars is to sit them on wooden blocks of the correct height, front and rear. This will work but will require readjustment of the bars after every movement of the frame.

Once the bars are in place, front and rear, a string should be run down each side of the car and through the holes at the end of each bar. Rather than tying the string at either end, a small weight should be tied at each end. This will keep the strings tight, allow for adjustment, and absorb an occasional accidental brushing of the string. This system of supports, bars, and strings can now be adjusted, as explained later, to form a perfect rectangle around the theoretical centerline of the car.

When making the supports, front and rear, allow for adjustments to compensate for the various tire size (hub heights) and ride height combinations that you can foresee. The bars should also be

6

as short as possible and still allow the strings to clear the widest possible track, wheel, and tire combination. When finally adjusted, the strings should pass just outboard of all four hubs within 1/4 inch vertically of the hub centers.

BUMP STEER PLATES

The bump steer plates are actually used to measure more than the usual toe change during bump and droop. If the car is being aligned without wheels, springs, and shocks, then the plates are used to provide a reference surface for measuring camber, castor, and individual wheel toe in.

Ideally, one should have a full complement of four plates and, as a minimum, two. The plates should be square, between 11 and 14 inches on a side and a minimum of 5/16 inch thick. They obviously must be perfectly flat with both sides parallel and all plates should be of exactly the same thickness. Since aluminum plate sells by the pound, it may be desirable to make four smaller plates. 6 x 14 inches is probably the smallest usable combination but may require rotating by 90 degrees for some measurements.

Once the size is determined, a large hole must be cut in the exact center of the plate to clear the usual hub protrusion found on most cars. Next, a bolt pattern must be drilled in the plate around the center hole such that the plate can be securely bolted to the hub. The plate should be mounted with its shortest dimension vertical. A series of parallel, horizontal lines should be scribed onto the plate starting with a line that passes through the center of the hub. A parallel line every 1 inch above and below the hub for a total of 3 inches in each direction should cover most normal suspension travel. The lines above the centerline are used to measure wheel droop, and those below to measure bump (see figure 2).

CAMBER GAUGE

There are a number of commercially offered camber gauges available selling for under $50.00. If you decide to purchase one, remember that most of your camber settings are going to be in the area of 0 to 1 degree and this range should have a minimum of 1/4 degree resolution. A slightly slower but much cheaper method of measuring camber is with a string and plumb bob. The string is either hung over the top of the bump steer plate or suspended slightly outboard of the wheel and tire. In either case, the distance of the string from the plate or wheel is measured at the top and bottom and the difference is proportional to the camber.

CAMBER DEG =ARCSIN (DIFF/VERT)

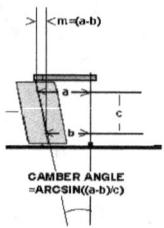

Where DIFF is the difference between the top and bottom distances from the strings, and VERT is the vertical distance between readings.
(Refer to figures 2 and 3.)

If a nominal 13 inch wheel is on the car then the vertical distance from the wheel's top and bottom lip surface will be around 14 inches. If a vertical string is suspended outboard of the wheel and tire (not touching either) and the string is 2 inches from the wheel at the top and 1 & 15/16 inches at the bottom then the camber is: ARCSIN[(1/16)/14]=.26. The fact that the string is closer at the bottom denotes negative camber. As a rule of thumb every 1/16 inch difference top and bottom is equal to 1/4 degree of camber on a 13 inch wheel.

When a string is suspended from the top of a bump steer plate, the plate should be rotated such that a vertical distance 14 inches below the highest point can be measured. When dealing with negative camber readings, the string must be suspended inboard of the plate. In this case, the string should be draped over the plate

8

such that the top horizontal distance to the string is always zero. Therefore, at a point 14 inches down on the plate, the camber can be directly read as multiples of 1/16 inches and easily converted to degrees.

If the string touches the plate at the bottom with this setup, then the camber on that corner of the car is zero or positive. The string must therefore be suspended outboard and the procedure repeated.

TOE BAR

Although the individual toe in (or out) of a particular wheel is measured using the parallel strings down the side of the car, occasionally it is desirable to make a quick check of the total front or rear toe. This method can be used to reset the toe on a single corner after some or all of its suspension has been replaced. For example, if the right rear were intact, the left rear corner could be repaired, assuming the right rear toe was still correct. The total toe could be set by making adjustments on the left side. This should bring the left rear individual toe back to its correct value. A device for measuring the total toe is simple to make. A 2 x 2 of relatively good quality wood and about the length of the widest end of the car can be fitted with two adjustable vertical pointers about half the height of your average tire diameter (see figure 6).

The bar is laid on the ground, horizontally, in front of the tires and the pointers aligned with a circumferential scribe mark on each tire. This scribe mark can be made by holding a sharp punch against the tire while rotating it. It is not necessary that the scribe marks be centered on the tire but they must continue completely and accurately around the tire.

Once the pointers have been aligned to the scribe marks in front of the tire, the entire bar with pointers should be carefully moved

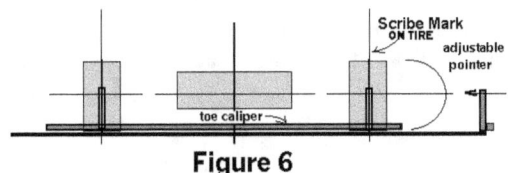

Figure 6

to the rear of the tire. The bar should be positioned such that the pointer on one side is aligned with the tire scribe mark. The difference between the pointer and the scribe mark on the other tire is the actual toe value. If the distance between the scribe marks at the front is shorter than at the rear then the wheels are toed in.

CASTOR GAUGE

As with the camber gauge, a castor gauge may be purchased, perhaps even in combination with a camber gauge. However, even if you are using strings to measure camber, the castor at each front corner can be computed from two camber readings.

From the straight ahead position (equal toe left front and right front) the steering should be turned a fixed distance to the left (approximately 15 degrees). The camber of both front wheels should be noted and a mark made on the steering rack (in order to repeat the measurement the next time). Next, the steering should be turned the same amount in the opposite direction (this is easily done by noting the rack travel to the left and moving the rack the same distance to the right. Again, note the camber of both wheels. The castor, at a given wheel, is the total angular camber change at the wheel times 2. Normally, one of the camber readings will be positive and one negative. In this case, the total angular difference is the sum of the two numbers disregarding which is positive and which is negative. In all cases, the castor is the arithmetic difference between the two numbers times 2.

RACK LOCKS

The position of the steering rack and housing relative to the suspension is an often overlooked item in suspension alignment. If the joints at either end of the rack are not positioned each the same distance from the theoretical chassis centerline, the toe in adjustment, camber change curves, and particularly the bump steer will produce a different action on both sides. Refer to figures 1 and 3. Once the centerline of the car is defined by the parallel strings, a measurement can be taken to center the steering rack. The distance from the steering rack clevis joints to the parallel

10

strings must be measured. The left and right distances should be made the same by turning the steering wheel as required. If the installation will allow, the steering rack housing can also be shifted, left or right, until centered. The advantage of this later method is that all subsequent measurements of the clevis positions can be made relative to the rack housing. There are several methods of keeping the rack in position throughout the alignment. The simplest of these is to scribe a mark on the rack itself and bolt a pointer on the frame to align with this mark. This method will still require constant adjustment as the rack is moved or bumped.

If the rack and housing are of suitable design and material, a small hole can be drilled through the housing into the rack. A pin can then be inserted to hold the rack in place. Two other holes could be drilled in the rack for setting the castor. One hole represents 15 degrees of steering to the left and the other hole represents 15 degrees to the right. All holes should be deburred and no deeper in the rack than absolutely necessary. When all else fails, hose clamps can be used to hold the rack against the fixed part of the housing. For all of the above methods, it will probably be necessary to move or remove the steering rack boots.

RIDE HEIGHT BLOCKS

An assortment of blocks and shims will be required to support the chassis at the correct ride height when the road springs and dampers are removed. The blocks should run the full width of the frame. Alternatively, one block can be used on each corner.

The next problem is how to support the suspension at each corner with the wheels and tires removed. Again, wooden blocks can be used and adjusted until the center of the hub at each corner is at exactly one-half of the tire diameter being used at that corner. Actually, the hub height at each corner should be directly measured in advance with the car ready to run, fully loaded with fuel and driver, and the tires at the correct inflation pressure. Refer to figures 1 and 2.

A very useful alternate method of maintaining the desired hub center height requires the fabricating of four dummy shock absorbers (see figure 2). A left- and a right-hand rod end can be threaded into the ends of a short piece of tubing or bar stock in such a way that the whole assembly can be installed between the upper and lower shock mounting points. By rotating the bar, the hub height can be easily adjusted.

In either case, the difference between the hub center height and the ride height defines the suspension geometry angles and it is this difference that must remain constant (see figure 3). If the tire size changes and/or the ride height changes (fuel burn off, etc.), then ideally, the spring platforms should be adjusted to give the hub-to-ride height difference at which the car was aligned.

Care must also be taken to avoid drastically altering the front-to-rear ride height difference (rake). Actually, all of these measurements can and should be changed during testing sessions. However, the amount of change relative to the point at which the chassis was aligned should be noted along with other pertinent test information.

MISCELLANEOUS TOOLS

In addition to the above tools it is usually necessary to have a 12 foot tape measure, a 3 to 4 foot level, a 6 inch pocket rule graduated in 32nds of an inch, and an adjustable 1 foot square.

Obviously, you also need a full complement of wrenches, etc., to make the necessary adjustments to the suspension links and other associated pieces.

III. SETUP PROCEDURE

The initial setup procedure is the most time-consuming part of the alignment. The accuracy with which you are able to measure all of the suspension parameters will depend entirely on how accurately your reference strings and plates are set up. With a little experience, you will learn which setup adjustments are critical and which do not require accurate setting. For example, it is of prime importance to have your reference strings exactly the same distance, left and right, from your chosen reference points on the plates. However, it is probably reasonable to eyeball the parallelness of the horizontal support bars, fore and aft. An out-of-parallel condition for the support bars of 1 inch at the end of the 72 inch bars will cause the reference strings to be out of parallel by less than 1/128th of an inch.

The accuracy of the ride height and hub height is relatively important. At the track, the ride height can normally be measured and controlled within 1/8th of an inch.

Although the reference strings should be close to the hub height, both front and rear, this measurement is probably not critical to within 1/2 inch. The fore and aft bars should be adjusted level to within 1/8th inch, left to right. This is the same as specifying that the strings be the same height from the floor at the left hub as at the right hub. The remainder of this section describes a sequential procedure for setting up the alignment equipment and explains some of the problems and alternatives you may encounter.

DETERMINE WHAT YOU WANT

Another often overlooked step in the alignment procedure is a careful determination of the suspension settings with which you wish to end up. Determining this at the onset can greatly reduce the amount of work and number of adjustments. There are many things that may influence the parameter selection, including:

- on track experience
- change in weight bias
- change in tire height or width

- aerodynamic balance changes
- expected track conditions
- new spring or swaybar rates

Although I promised not to get into the subject of what things produce specific handling characteristics, I am going to present a list of cause and effect relationships that some persons feel hold true some of the time. These are, by no means, absolutes and you should not be afraid to adjust in exactly the opposite direction. Assuming that the handling of your car is not a perfect balance between oversteer and understeer, the "loose" end might stick better (be brought back into balance) by adjusting the following at that end.

- Increase negative camber.
- Soften the swaybar.
- Install softer springs.
- Install wider tires.
- Install better tires.
- Increase tire pressure.
- Lower the ride height.
- Add toe in on bump.
- Increase the aerodynamic down force.
- Increase the camber-change rate.
- Drive slower.

Theoretically, the opposite can be performed at the "good" end of the car but this is usually a step backwards in overall cornering power. Always try to make the "loose" end stick better.

For experimentation purposes, it is probably a good idea to make a relatively large change in only one item at a time. This will more readily point out any change in handling. For last minute pre-race adjustments, it is better to make small changes in a known direction or to leave well enough alone.

After carefully considering all of the above and comparing them with any previous alignment specifications that you have, the following values should be determined:

- front castor or bump specifications
- front camber (degrees positive or negative)
- front toe (inches per wheel, IN or OUT)
- front ride height (inches to frame)
- front hub height (half the tire diameter)
- rear castor or bump specifications
- rear camber (degrees per wheel)
- rear toe (inches per wheel, IN or OUT)
- rear ride height (inches to frame)
- rear hub height (half the tire diameter)

PLACE ON LEVEL BLOCKS

Next, the car should be placed on a level surface in exactly the same

position that it was last aligned. Taped squares on the floor are good for marking the location. Refer to figure 1.

LEVELING SYSTEM

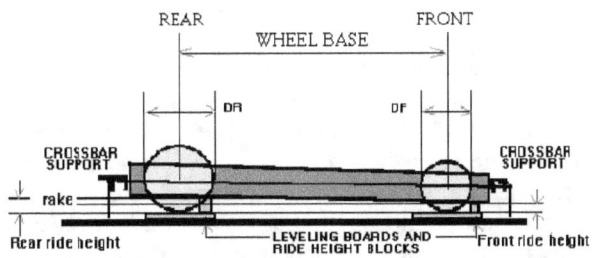

Figure 1

Two ride height blocks for the front and two for the rear should be fabricated and placed under each corner of the frame at the same reference point as when last aligned.

Remove one link from both the front and rear swaybars.

Carefully remove one or both bolts from each shock absorber/spring unit. Normally, the lower shock mounting bolts can be removed and the top bolt left in place. In any case, the car should then be lowered on to the ride height blocks with no interference from the shock/spring assembly. Remember that during the bump steer operation, the suspension must be raised and lowered the full extent of its travel. If it appears that any of the four corners will interfere with the shock, then now is the time to completely remove the entire unit. If dummy shocks are going to be used (see below), then the shocks are going to be removed in any case.

Since the wheels and tires are now supporting the hubs only (i.e. not the chassis), now is a good time to install either the dummy shocks between the upper and lower shock mounting points or the hub height support blocks. If dummy shocks are not used, then the front and rear suspension must be supported by these blocks before removing the wheels.

Next, remove all four wheels and tires and adjust the hub center height at all four corners to the previously determined value. Note that the front wheels should be as close to straight ahead as possible.

At this point, it may be desirable to install the steering rack locks. If the steering rack has been previously centered, then installing the locks should force the front wheels straight ahead. If the rack is not centered or the wheels are not straight ahead (due to a shunt etc.), then a preliminary toe adjustment should be made with the toe bar and pointers. The purpose of this exercise is to put the hubs in the proper orientation so that the hub height and string position will not change drastically when the toe is later adjusted more accurately.

The rear toe should also be set approximately correct for the same reason. All of this should only be necessary if the car is badly out of alignment. Normally, small suspension changes will have little effect on the hub height. At any rate, the hub height along with everything else should be periodically checked throughout the alignment.

At this point, we have the hub center height and ride height differences mechanically defined. It is this relationship that defines the static angles of all of the suspension links.

BUMP STEER PLATES

Next, the bump steer plates should be affixed to as many corners of the car as possible. If only two plates are available, then initially the plates should be placed at the rear and some other reference point chosen at the front (e.g. front brake rotor). A single reference point on all four plates should be determined and marked for measurement to the reference strings. A point as close to the hub center as possible should be used. For example, such a reference point could be a flat surface to the front of, and below, the hub center on all four wheels. This point should be used for all adjustments of the string reference lines.

PARALLEL STRING INSTALLATION

The front and rear crossbar supports should next be installed along with the crossbars and fore-aft strings. Refer to figures 1 and 4. The bars should be adjusted until they are level and such that they support the parallel strings at the correct hub height, front and rear. The front and rear crossbars should be reasonably parallel to each other. The latter can be done by measuring from each end of a bar to a common suspension or frame point on the left and right sides of the car. For example, the distance from the top front ball joint forward to the crossbar should be the same left and right. Next, the strings must be equidistant from the plate reference points at the front and equidistant at the rear. This requirement means that the left front reference distance will equal the right front reference distance. The rear reference distances must be equal but not necessarily equal to those at the front. These reference distances are adjusted by shifting the crossbars left or right. Remember that a shift at the front changes both the front and rear distances. As this adjustment is made, care must be taken not to change the string height or crossbar angular orientation.

The adjustment of these strings is the single most important item affecting accuracy. For this reason, the string reference distances

PARALLEL STRING SYSTEM

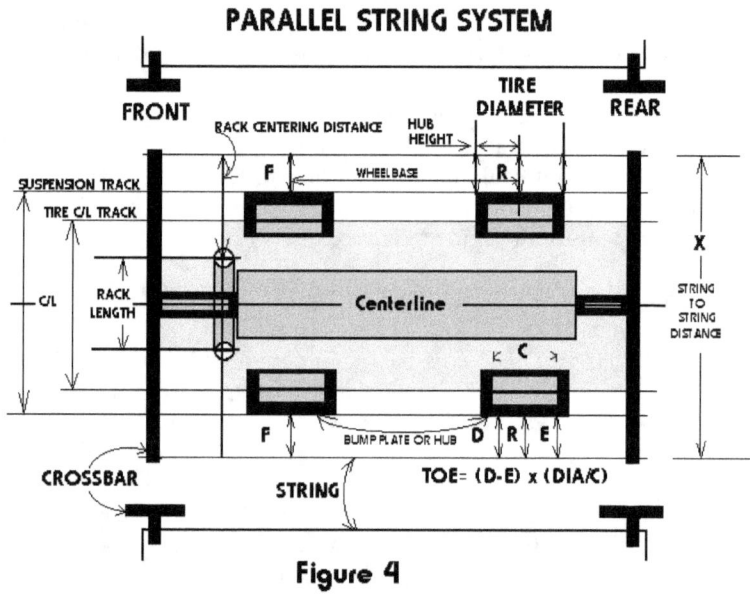

TOE= (D-E) x (DIA/C)

Figure 4

should be checked and readjusted as necessary after each suspension adjustment. There will be little, if any, actual adjustment required if the car is relatively close to the desired alignment. If the car has never been aligned or appears to be severely out-of-spec, then more effort will be required to keep the strings parallel to the car centerline.

An underlying assumption that allows this scheme to work, is that each corner of the car has a theoretically fixed length suspension piece that determines the track and therefore, the centerline of the car. At the rear, this is almost always the forward link of the lower wishbone or parallel arm assembly. The distance between the outboard (at the upright) and the inboard (at the frame) joint of this wishbone leg should be the same, left and right, and only adjusted in pairs if a track adjustment is required. The third joint on the wishbone (on the rear leg) is used only to adjust the toe value at that wheel. At the front, the lower wishbone is treated in much the same way except in cases where another suspension link is obviously not adjustable and whose length is obviously set at the factory. This is typically the case for a front suspension with upper rocker arm geometry. With this layout, the rocker remains fixed and all other adjustments are made with the lower wishbone links.

Since this assumption produces a fixed reference distance between the upright pickup point and the frame pickup point, then all else being equal (i.e. camber, castor, and toe), the strings will be parallel to the chassis centerline as defined by the frame pickup points of these fixed length links.

> **Note that as the camber is adjusted at one corner, the plate reference point at that corner moves in or out, as does the centerline of the car.**

Therefore, the strings must be moved to follow the hub (plate reference points).

If the frame was perfect in regard to the location of each pickup point, then, as the camber adjustment at the left moved the centerline one direction, the camber adjustment at the right would move it back, etc. The fact of the matter is that no frame is as close in dimension as we are trying to set the suspension parameters. If it was, first of all, it would never remain that way. Secondly, no suspension aligning would be necessary since the geometry could be calculated by the length of the links. For example, a rear camber link of 8 inches would always give the correct camber as designed in at the factory. Obviously, this will never hold true in actual practice.

WHAT SETTINGS DO YOU HAVE

The next step is to measure the castor, camber and toe at the front and rear and note what you have. If the basic alignment is in doubt, a cursory check of the bump steer curves will also be in order. The left and right wheel base should also be measured.

IV. ADJUSTMENT

Having the above information to compare with your desired settings, a line of attack can be determined that should minimize your efforts. Unfortunately, this determination will also be based largely on experience. The second time through this procedure will, however, be easier only if the first time has been adequately documented. Besides noting how many turns of a camber link produces a degree of camber change, it should also be noted how much this change altered castor, toe, etc. With a little experience and common sense, it is occasionally possible to effect two changes in the right direction with a single adjustment. For example, adding negative camber may also produce the extra toe out you were looking for.

When in doubt the following adjustment sequence should be a good place to start.

- track
- wheel base
- castor
- camber
- toe
- bump steer
- repeat all of the above as required

Some general comments on the making of the actual adjustments are in order at this point. First of all, you should locate all left-hand thread rod ends and mark them with paint or tape. When shortening or lengthening a suspension link with a left-hand thread at one end and a right-hand thread at the other, you should first unlock both jam nuts and back them off a good distance.

Next, focus your attention on the right-hand thread. The direction to rotate the link to shorten or lengthen it should then be obvious.

When the adjustment is complete you should probably still leave the jam nuts free. The probability is quite good that some other adjustment will change what you have just done. When all adjustments have been made on the car, you should systematically inspect and tighten every jam nut and every suspension bolt on the car.

When tightening a jam nut be very careful not to turn the suspension link and thus undo what you have just spent hours on. This will not be a problem if both ends of the link have right-hand threads. However, the disadvantage of this arrangement is that the link must be completely removed at one end every time an adjustment is made. After the jam nuts are tight, the link should rotate freely within the confines of the pickup point clevises. If there is little or no clearance for rotation, the jam nuts should be slackened and the rod ends adjusted at both ends to allow for maximum rotational clearance. Again, be careful not to turn the actual suspension link further than the few degrees needed to produce the clearance.

TRACK

As mentioned previously, the track may not be an adjustable item at both ends of the car. Although the distance between tire centers can be changed by using wheel spacers and various offset wheels, this is not truly an adjustment of track as it references the suspension geometry. Significant variations in handling can be produced by using different offset wheels. This is due mainly to the relationship of the suspension to the tire contact patch, which can change the affective wheel rate, and steering axis intersection with the contact patch.

In any case, for our purposes the track is the distance between the farthest outboard fixed-machined surface of the suspension on one side, and its counterpart on the other side (see figure 4). Since this surface is the hub face in virtually all cases, the wheel offset and spacers being used can be added to arrive at the tire center-to-center measurement normally referred to as track. The suspension track, as we shall call it, is usually set at the factory by jigging a fixed suspension piece at each corner. Unless that piece is bent (accidentally or deliberately), the track should not change. Therefore, the track on your car can be checked by directly measuring the length of these fixed suspension components and comparing these findings with the factory specifications. If factory specs are unavailable, then a good place to start is by making the left component equal in length to the right one. Even though these fixed components are jig set at the factory, most come with rod ends for adjustment to compensate for manufacturing errors. If yours does not have this adjustment, as in the case of some rocker arm suspension units, then you can either bend the one you have into shape, buy a new one, or live with it. The latter may be quite acceptable if the error is not large, say 1/4 inch. The alignment procedure described here is designed to average out such errors as best as possible.

WHEEL BASE

The next item to be checked is wheel base. Here again, it is not as important that the wheel base be a specific value as that it be equal, left and right.

With the wheels and tires off and the chassis supported by blocks and dummy shocks, the actual wheel base is easily measured from the front to the rear hub center (see figure 4). Note that the wheel base will change as other suspension parameters are adjusted. Toe and castor adjustments will significantly alter the wheel base. In any case, the wheel base must be checked with the steering rack locked in the straight ahead position. If the position of the front steering is in question, an alternate, preliminary method of checking wheel base can be used. A machined surface on the front and rear suspension should be chosen and a measurement taken between the two. For example, at the front, the center of the upper ball joint or the edge of its housing can be used. At the rear, the leading edge of the upright at the top can be used or the center of an adjacent pickup on the upright. The number obtained from this measurement is not the actual wheel base but is directly related to wheel base.

22

The wheel base should be equally maintained, left and right, to about 1/8 inch. If you find a drastic discrepancy in your left and right measurements, then the wheel base should be adjusted at this point. The wheel base can either be lengthened on the short side or shortened on the long side. Before deciding which way to go, carefully examine the amount of adjustment remaining on the rod ends of the rear trailing arms. Also, check the angles of both rear half shafts relative to the suspension. Except in extreme cases, it is probably easiest and best to adjust the wheel base at the rear as opposed to the front. The actual adjustment is made by shortening or lengthening both trailing arms on one side by the same amount. This adjustment should move the half shaft towards a more perpendicular exit from the gearbox. It is, of course, also necessary to leave enough threads on all rod ends for adjustment and safety.

CASTOR

Castor is the fore-aft tilt (angle) of the hub carrier or upright at each corner of the car. At the front, this angle is formed by the line that the upper and lower ball joints make with the vertical. At the rear, it is normally measured as the angle that the lower wishbone outboard pickup points make with the horizontal. The tops of the front uprights are normally leaned back (positive castor) and the tops of the rear uprights are normally leaned forward (negative castor). However, adjusting the bump steer may produce strange rear castor angles.

At the front, the castor can be measured by taking two camber readings at each wheel. The first is taken with the wheel at a fixed angular distance in one direction (say 15 degrees) and the second, with the wheel the same angular distance in the opposite direction. The total angular camber difference times 2 is the castor at that wheel. A castor gauge can be purchase to measure much the same thing but both methods should give the angle of the upper and lower ball joints to vertical.

The castor is adjusted by altering the length of the upper or lower trailing arm. The effect is to push or pull the top or bottom of the upright in the direction needed to increase or decrease the castor angle. If, for example, the front suspension has a lower trailing arm from the lower ball joint rearward to the frame, then lengthening this link will push the bottom of the front upright forward. The net effect of this is to increase the angle that the top and bottom ball joints make with the vertical.

While the leaning back of the front upright produces a larger castor angle, it also increases the ride height change with steering angle change.

With zero castor at the front, each hub would be free to turn about a vertical reference line. Since this reference line has been leaned back somewhat, the hub must now move up and down as well as left and right around this line. The natural tendency is for the weight of the car to resist this downward motion of the hub (upward frame motion). This resistance is in balance with the steering centered and with the left and right castor equal. The larger the castor angle becomes, the longer the lever becomes that the weight of the car has to work with. Thus, there will be a greater resistance for the steering to leave the straight ahead position. Therefore, the steering becomes heavier with larger castor angles.

Another effect of front castor is an increase in negative camber at the outside wheel in a turn. This usually means that the tighter the turn is, the more negative camber the outside front wheel will have. At the rear, the castor measure is mainly used as a starting reference point for bump steer adjustment. A good place to start is with both sides equal and about zero. If wheel base, camber, and toe are equal, left and right, then the castor angle obtained in adjusting the bump steer at one side should be the same as will be found when adjusting the other side.

The rear castor is usually adjusted by lengthening or shortening the top trailing arm. This is also the same link used to adjust the bump steer. Although the lower link can be used to adjust the castor, it will also drastically alter the toe value which will subsequently have to be readjusted using the outboard rear wishbone joint. This is probably acceptable if enough adjustment exists in all the links involved. Since the wheel base adjustment also involves the rear trailing arms, the rear castor and wheel base can and should be done at the same time. Here, as usual, the lengths and angles must be juggled until the wheel base and castor are equal, left and right. In the case of castor, your previous knowledge of where the best bump steer occurs will help. If, for example, the wheel base is correct and you arbitrarily set the castor at zero, then during bump steer, you could find out that two degrees of castor are required. This would require significantly altering the length of the top rear trailing arm (hopefully the same amount on both sides). This change in the top trailing arms will alter the wheel base. If the new wheel base is equal, left and right, and the half shafts are at an acceptable angle, then there is no problem. If, however, the wheel base is unacceptable for some reason, then the top and bottom links must be adjusted to produce an acceptable wheel base at this new castor angle. Hopefully, all of this will not require too much readjustment of other things but it usually does. Had you known the approximate rear castor angle to start with, all of the above mentioned adjustments would probably not have been needed. The bump steer would require little castor change which would, therefore, require little, if any, wheel base adjustment, etc..

The best method of measuring rear castor is by placing a small carpenter's square fore-aft across the outboard end of the lower wishbone. A camber gauge can then be used to measure the angle of the vertical member of the square. If you don't have a camber gauge, a good level can be laid across the wishbone at this same point. The position of the bubble can be noted, compared to previous experience and compared to the reading at the other side of the car. After all, the absolute castor reading is of little importance for our application.

CAMBER

Wheel camber is usually measured in degrees, and refers to the angle that the wheel makes with the vertical. Negative camber refers to the condition where the tops of the tires are closer to the center of the car than the bottoms. Positive camber is, of course, the reverse situation where the tops of the tires lean away from the

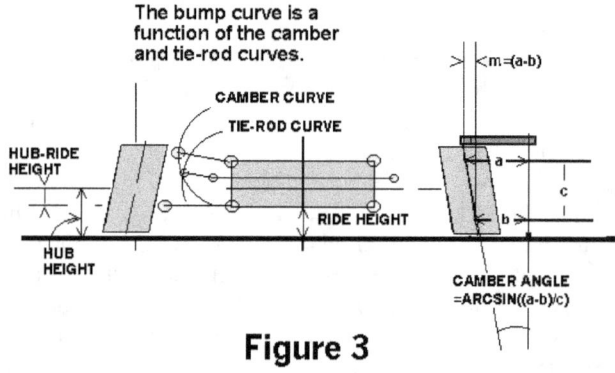

Figure 3

car. The trend seems to be to use a small amount of negative camber as a starting point for suspension evaluation (0 to .5 degrees negative).

There are several reasons for running any negative camber at all, as opposed to having the tire flat on the ground. Negative camber can be used to cause the tires to produce a "camber thrust" that resists movement of the car to the outside of the turn. A predetermined amount of negative camber is also necessary on some suspension to prevent the tire from developing positive camber as the chassis rolls under cornering loads.

Also, if the camber curve is properly designed, the tire can be maintained in a fixed relationship with the level track surface even though the chassis may roll several degrees.

A camber curve can be measured and plotted the same as the bump steer. The curve can also be altered in several ways depending on chassis design. Suppose that a given negative going camber curve is plotted for a wheel at 0, 1, 2 and 3 inches of bump and it is determined that more negative camber change is desired. A lot of this discussion will vary depending on the suspension layout, but typically, a single camber control link can be found that angles from the frame upward and out to the top of the upright. This single link should control the camber unless the lower wishbone links are greatly out of parallel with the level surface of the ground. This later situation should normally be avoided as it can have some very abrupt effects on handling as the chassis rolls. For example, if the lower wishbone was angled outward and down from the frame a large amount then under wheel bump in cornering the rear track will widen as the chassis rolls. This is not usually very conducive to stick.

In most cases, with level lower links, the top camber control link pickup points can be adjusted to alter the camber curves. The more this link angles upward and outward, the faster the camber will move negative during wheel bump (i.e. chassis roll to the outside in a turn). Refer to figure 2.

At the front, this camber link angle can usually be changed by adding spacers between the link and the top of the front upright. At the rear, a bracket or new pickup point must usually be fabricated. It is, however, interesting to note that lowering the frame at one end of the car will usually increase the static negative camber and place the suspension on a faster section of the camber curve. Lowering the frame effectively increases the angle of the camber link as previously discussed.

The static ride height camber at either end of the car is adjusted to its nominal value by lengthening the camber link to go more positive or shortening it to go more negative.

If you have a camber gauge it can be held against the bump plate as close to the hub center as possible and the camber angle read directly. If you want to use a plumb bob and string it should be allowed to hang vertically from the top horizontal edge. Normally for negative camber, the string will be suspended to the inboard side of the plate. At a point 14 inches from the top of the plate the distance of the string from the plate in inches times 4 is the camber in degrees. This method can also be implemented by suspending a string and weight outboard of an installed wheel and tire. The difference in string distance from the top wheel lip and bottom wheel lip times 4 is the camber in degrees. Again, the vertical distance between readings should be 14 inches, which is about the distance, edge-to-edge, on a 13 inch wheel.

TOE

The toe in of a wheel can be measured relative to the centerline of the car (individual toe) or relative to the opposite wheel (total toe). The latter method is normally sufficient for passenger car front end alignment. For our purposes, the total toe is only used as a starting point when assembling a car or corner of a car. The total toe can easily be measured using a large caliper made from a long bar with two 10 to 12 inch vertical pointers (see figure 6).

The only complication involved in using the toe caliper is the scribing of circumferential lines around each tire. Although these lines are usually scribed near the center of each tire, this is not an accuracy requirement. The only requirement is that wherever the scribe line starts it ends up at the same place with no deviations in between.

Once the scribe marks are made, one need only set the caliper to the scribe marks at one end of the tire and then by moving the caliper to the other side, compare the front to rear scribe marks. If the marks are closer together at the front, then the total toe is in the "IN" direction. This method can be used at the front or rear of the car.

The total toe can be used to set an individual wheel toe if the opposite wheel has a known accurate individual toe value. For example, assume the left front corner was damaged and components replaced but the right front was still intact. Assume the car was originally aligned with 1/16th inch toe in at each wheel. Now, if the total toe in is set at 1/8th using the toe caliper, and all adjustments are made at the left tie-rod, then the left wheel toe will be 1/16th inch. This same procedure works at the rear.

During a complete alignment check, however, it is important to individually adjust each wheel to the chassis centerline. This is especially critical at the rear where there is no steering wheel to correct for a small toe adjustment mistake. If the rear total toe is correct but all of the toe is at one side and perhaps the opposite side is actually toed the wrong way, relative to the chassis centerline, then some very peculiar handling characteristics could result.

At the front, the individual wheel toe is still important, if the bump steer and camber curves are to behave similarly, left and right. However, these factors are not quite as sensitive to left to right toe error as at the rear. At the front, the actual left to right toe can be maintained equal with steering adjustments, while only the bump and camber curves suffer.

At any rate, since the same parallel string setup used to check the rear wheel toe can be used to check the front, there is no reason not to set the individual front wheel toe.

Once the parallel strings and crossbars are installed and their front and rear reference distances set up, the toe can be measured at any wheel by measuring the distance of the string from the front and from the rear of the bump plates (see figure 4). If the string is closer to the plate at the front of a given wheel than the rear then that corner is toed out. The actual fore-aft distance across the plate between the readings must be known to convert the string difference number to toe at the tire surface.

TOE IN =
(Tire Diameter/The Distance Between Readings) x The Difference In Readings

For a plate half the width of a tire diameter, your difference reading must be multiplied by 2 to reflect the actual toe at the tire.

The toe can be computed in degrees the same as camber. If the difference readings are taken 14 inches apart, then the toe (in degrees) is 4 times the difference. This toe check at the front is only possible due to the steering rack being locked in a centered position. That is, the clevis joints at the ends of the rack are the same distance from the chassis centerline.

As with all adjustments, the parallel string reference distances must be checked and adjusted as needed after each toe adjustment.

The actual toe in or out adjustment is made at the front by lengthening or shortening the tie-rods which usually contain a left and right-hand rod end, or a right-hand rod end and a ball joint. If the steering rack is located in front of the front axle, then shortening this tie-rod will cause that corner of the car to toe in. If the bump steer is in question at any particular corner, then it is probably not worth fussing with the final toe value. If the toe is within a 1/16 inch of the desired value, then note its value and recheck after doing the bump steer.

At the rear, the toe is usually adjusted by lengthening or shortening the rear outboard lower wishbone link. Lengthening this link pushes the bottom rear of the upright away from the centerline of the car. This has the effect of causing toe in on that corner. Recheck the strings at this point. The toe can also be adjusted by changing the length of the lower trailing arm but this should not be used unless you run out of adjustment elsewhere. Changing the length of the lower trailing arm will alter too many other things like wheel base and castor.

BUMP STEER

Bump steer is a measure of how much the static toe value changes as the wheel moves through its range of vertical travel relative to the frame. This vertical travel is referred to as bump when the wheel moves up relative to the frame and droop when the wheel moves down relative to the frame. The static toe is the reference value that occurs when the car is at the aligned ride and hub height.

A typical chassis in cornering will have the outside suspension in bump (due to chassis roll and weight transfer) and the inside suspension in droop (relatively unloaded). For this reason, the wheel bump relative to the static suspension setting is usually more important than wheel droop.

Although bump steering a suspension implies "dialing" in a certain amount of toe in, or toe out change with chassis roll, it is usual practice to adjust all toe change out of suspension bump. Thus, the toe value remains known regardless of the amount of chassis roll, and one less unknown in this business is surely of some value. Zero bump steer also allows you to adjust ride height without fear of changing the toe in. Another plus! After track testing of the chassis, it may be desirable to dial in a known amount roll oversteer or roll understeer. Roll oversteer is produced by toe out on bump at the rear or toe in on bump at the front. Roll understeer is produced by toe out on bump at the front

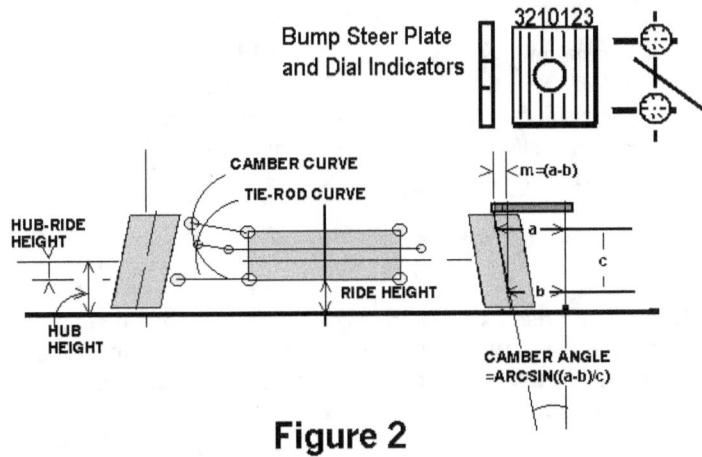

Figure 2

and toe in on bump at the rear.

Whatever you decide to try, you must be able to accurately measure it. Since what we want to know is the amount of toe change during bump, we can theoretically move the suspension incrementally up and down and measure the toe value relative to the strings in the usual fashion. The investment in two inexpensive dial indicators will make this job much easier and much more informative since the continuous (not incremental) changes in toe can be seen. Especially at the front, the toe characteristics can reverse at certain positions of bump and droop. This is because of the different arcs that the camber control link and tie-rod link travel through. Refer to figure 3.

The two dial indicators can be mounted on a fabricated stand that holds them at opposite ends of the bump plates. Their push rods should be horizontal against the plate at the hub centerline scribed on the plate and labeled as zero. The indicators should be preloaded to about half their travel (.5 inches if they are 1 inch indicators). Next, the dials on the indicator faces should be zeroed. At this point, the actual toe change can be watched as the suspension is moved up (and down if droop is important). If the indicator at the front of the plate extends its pushrod faster than the one at the rear, then the suspension is toeing in on bump (or droop).

At the rear, the toe change rate is usually controlled by the top trailing arm length. The bottom arm can be used also but this usually results in significant static toe changes. Assuming a conventional suspension, the following should hold true for the rear suspension:

TO REDUCE TOE IN ON BUMP SHORTEN THE TOP TRAILING ARM
TO REDUCE TOE OUT ON BUMP LENGTHEN THE TOP TRAILING ARM

Once the correct bump steer has been achieved, be sure to note the rear castor angle for future reference. All else being equal, it is really the castor angle of the rear upright that determines the toe characteristics.

At the front, the toe change can tend to be more complicated depending on the steering rack location with respect to ride height. If the steering rack is located such that the tie-rods are level or slightly inclined to the outboard end and the camber control link is in a similar orientation, then for bump the toe curve should be easily adjustable. When the camber link and tie-rod are not angled the same way, or when one or the other makes a transition from being angled downward to the outside to upward, the toe curve can oscillate wildly. Usually, the outboard end of the tie-rod where it connects to the steering arm can be shimmed to make both links operate in the same arc.

In any case, this location must be shimmed to adjust the bump steer curves accurately. In some installations, it may be possible to shift the steering rack up and down to adjust bump steer. This is usually a much more complicated method especially when the left requires more adjustment than the right. Therefore, the vertical rack adjustment should be used to produce the above mentioned tie-rod angles and then shims used at the ends of the steering arms to adjust the bump steer curves.

The direction of adjustment at the front is easier to visualize than at the rear. Assume, for our discussions, that both the tie-rod and the upper camber link are angled upward to the outboard end. Assume also that the lower links are relatively level to the ground and therefore imparting little camber change. We can change the angle of the tie-rod by adding or removing spacers between it and the steering arm. Raising the outboard end of the tie-rod by adjusting spacers will increase the angle of the tie-rod. Increasing this angle will cause the steering arm to move inward further for the same vertical suspension travel (bump). Assuming the rack and therefore the tie-rods are in front of the upper camber link, then this faster inward movement will cause the front of the wheel to move inward faster during bump. The top camber link also pulls the rear top of the wheel in at a predetermined rate (camber curve). By adjusting the spacers at the tie-rod end and therefore adjusting the rate at the front of the tire, a combination can be found that moves the front in at the same rate as the rear. This will be the zero toe change we have been looking for.

In summary, for a front suspension whose top camber link and tie-rod are angled upward, with the steering rack to the front and with spacers on top of the steering arm (and thus under the outboard tie-rod joint), the following should hold.

ADDING SPACERS WILL REDUCE TOE OUT ON BUMP
REMOVING SPACERS WILL REDUCE TOE IN ON BUMP

As has been repeatedly emphasized, all adjustments should be followed by a cursory check of all other parameters. A little experience and a lot of notes can make this recheck a trivial operation.

V. FINISHING UP

When you are satisfied that all of the suspension is statically and dynamically set to your specifications be sure you accurately note all of the final numbers. It can be difficult a few weeks later to sift through a list of hurried notes. The following should be performed while the chassis is still on the level surface.

- INSTALL SWAY BARS WITH NO PRELOAD
- CORNER WEIGHTS
- SET RIDE HEIGHT WITH SPRING PLATFORMS

INSTALL SWAY BARS

This is a relatively simple operation but can often be overlooked and can cause problems. The sway bar link that was removed during the setup procedure should be adjusted in length so that it can be connected to the sway bar without twisting the bar. A link that is too long on one side or the other can jack the frame and cause a lot of suspension adjustment to be wasted.

This should be done front and rear before the springs and shocks are installed. The frame and hub heights must be at their correct static position.

CORNER WEIGHTS

Before reinstalling the springs and shock absorbers, a measurement should be taken at all four corners between the upper and lower shock mounting point. This should be done with the frame and suspension in its static position as aligned. Theoretically, these measurements should be equal, left to right. If these numbers vary significantly then the spring platforms will probably have to be set differently, left and right, to compensate for the variation.

This shock length difference will probably also show up if the chassis corner weights are accurately checked (not bathroom scales). If the spring rates and lengths are equal, left and right, then the spring platform heights, left and right, can be set using the above shock length variation.

When measuring the height of a spring platform on a shock absorber be sure you are referencing an accurate surface on the shock. The threaded section of the shock body may vary from one shock to another. It is best to measure from the pickup point joint on the shock.

If the shock mounting point distances are known and compensated for, and the springs are of the same rate and length the chassis will usually have equal corner weights. If an unbalance is suspected, the first thing to check is the spring rates and lengths. If this checks out, the next step is to find a place to weigh all four corners at once. If each corner of the car does not weigh repeatedly the same, regardless of the chassis orientation on the scales, then you have not found the right place for checking corner weights.

The usual problem with bathroom scales is that the four corners are not at the same height when the weighing takes place. Even a minor deviation in scale height will cause large errors in measurement.

Most truck weigh stations are not calibrated to operate in the lower range we are interested in. Even if they are repeatable, they often also have the problem of providing a level surface between the corner being weighed and the rest of the car. In any case, don't start adjusting spring platforms until you are sure you have a repeatable measuring system.

When adjusting spring platforms to change corner weights, the frame should be raised on the light corner. This will make the light corner heavier and the diagonally opposite corner heavier.

When all of the above has been completed the ride height at either end of the chassis can be adjusted by moving the spring platforms up or down equally in pairs. This is true even if the platforms are not at the same height to start with. As with all alignment measurements, the relative difference in shock platforms, left and right, should be noted for future reference.

RIDE HEIGHT

As was discussed earlier, the chassis frame to ground clearance should be adjusted to the desired hub height to ride height difference. Obviously, fuel loads and tire sizes are going to vary this relationship. Perhaps even deliberate changes to this relationship can be beneficial. In any case, the place to start is with the hub height minus the frame (ride) height at the value determined at alignment time. Any changes in tire size or load should be noted in terms of this figure. At the next alignment session, these numbers and their effect on performance will determine possible new ride height to hub height ratios. Once a good combination is found don't be afraid to adjust the ride height before a qualifying session or race to compensate for a different fuel load.

VI. FIGURES

Figure 1 - Leveling System

LEVELING SYSTEM

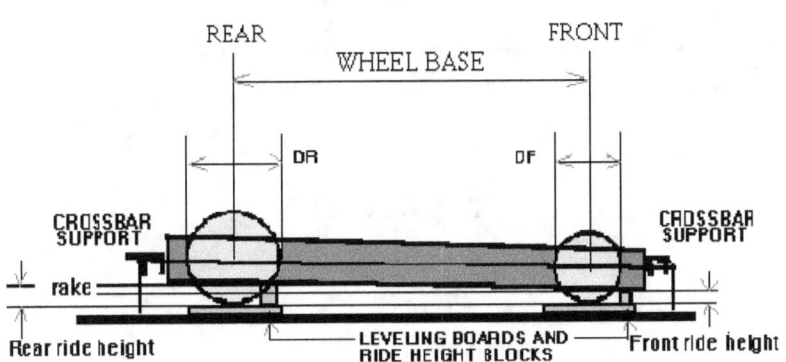

Figure 1

Figure 2 and Figure 3 – Bump Steer and Camber

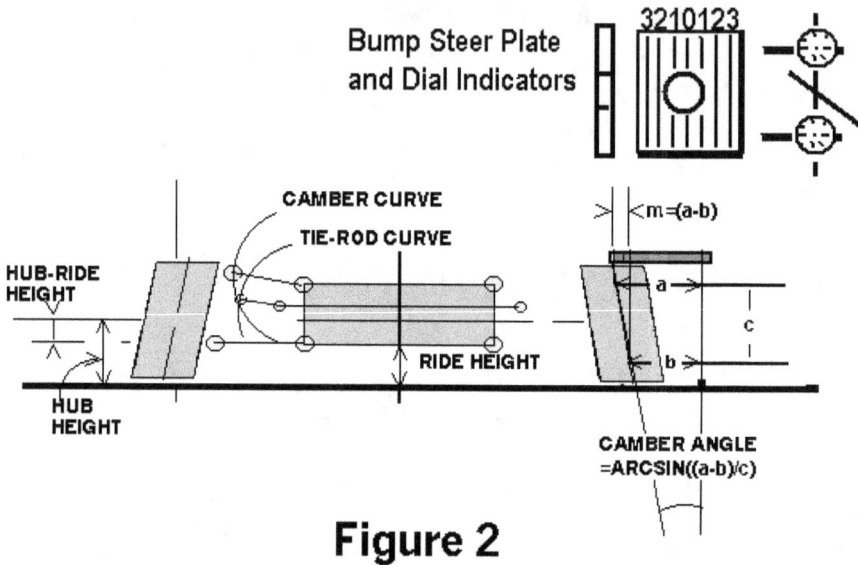

Figure 2

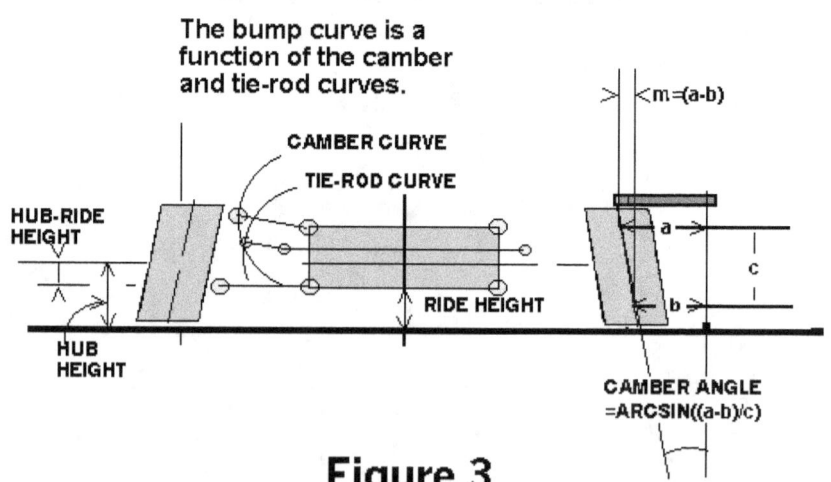

Figure 3

Figure 4 – Parallel Strings

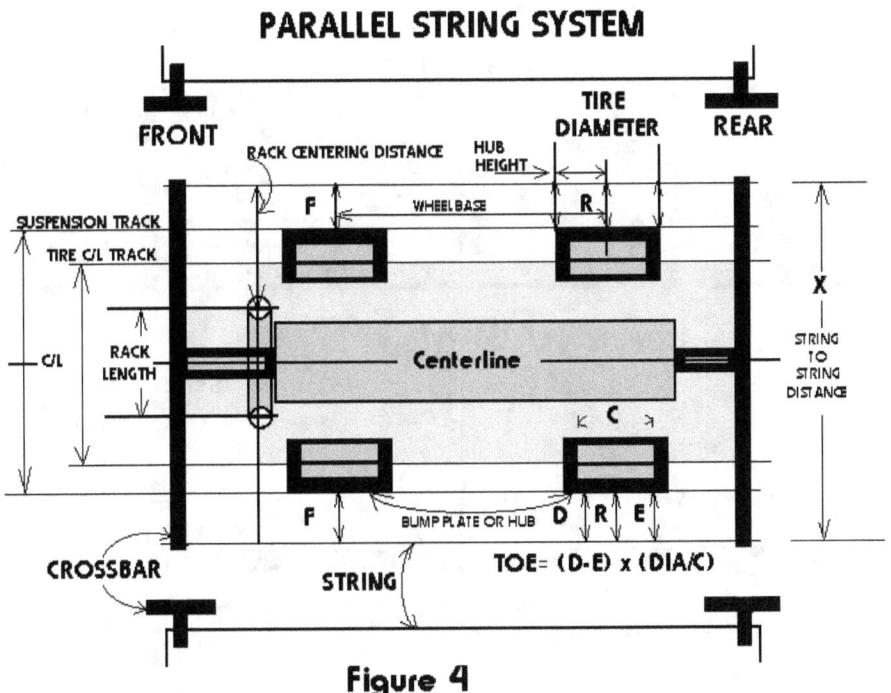

Figure 4

Figure 5 and Figure 6 – Ride Height

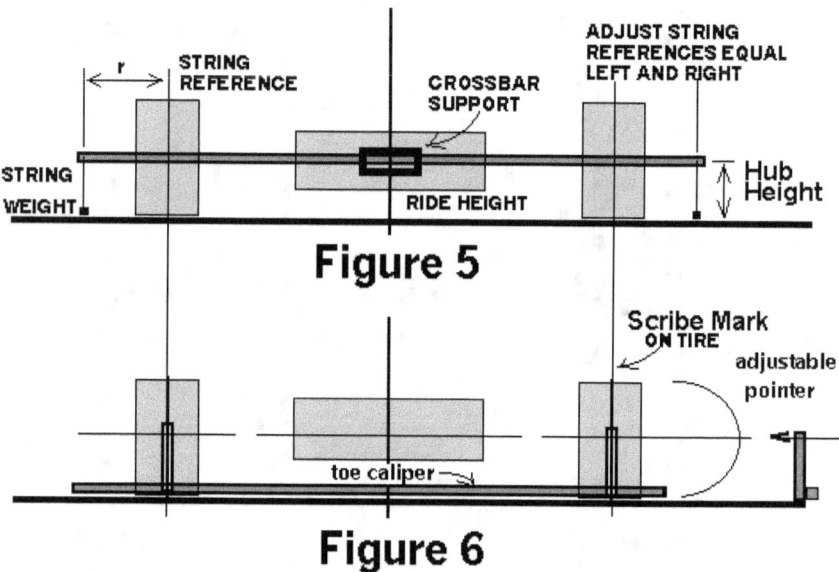

VII. ALIGNMENT WORKSHEETS

Date	
Chassis	

Desired Setting	Front	Rear	Comment
Ride Height	FRH=	RRH=	
Tire Circumference	CF=	CR=	
Hub Height	FHH=	RHH=	C x 0.159
Castor	FCAS=	RCAS=	Per Corner
Camber	FCAM=	RCAM=	Per Corner
Toe	FTOE=	RTOE=	Per Corner
Wheel Base	Left Side=	Right Side=	Left and Right
Track	FTRK=	RTRK=	

HUB HEIGHT = TIRE DIA/2 = TIRE CIRCUMFERENCE x 0.159

RIDE HEIGHT IS MEASURED
FROM (_____) AT THE FRONT,
AND (_____) AT THE REAR.

FRONT TRACK IS MEASURED FROM (_____)
REAR TRACK IS MEASURED FROM (_____)

WHEEL BASE IS MEASURED FROM
THE (_____) AT THE FRONT,
TO (_____) AT THE REAR.

FRONT HUB HEIGHT MINUS RIDE HEIGHT (FHH-FRH) = (___)
REAR HUB HEIGHT MINUS RIDE HEIGHT (RHH-RRH) = (___)

CASTOR CALCULATION FOR THE FRONT

	Left Front Camber	Right Front Camber
Wheels Left 15 Degrees		
Wheels Right 15 Degrees		
Difference (Left –Right)		
Times Two is Castor		

With the wheels a fixed distance (angle) to the left (about 15 degrees), measure the camber at the LF and RF. Repeat the readings with the wheels to the right, the same distance. The numerical difference in camber times two is the castor.

STATIC TOE

The static toe is measured with the car at the correct hub and ride height using the parallel string distances to the bump steer plates.

TOE = (TIRE DIAMETER/c)*(d-e)

WHERE: **c**=Front to rear distance between readings on the plate.
          d=Front reading. Distance from string to plate.
          e=Rear reading. Distance from string to plate.

          If **d** is larger than **e** then the wheel is toed IN.
          If **d** is less than **e** then the wheel is toed OUT.
          E.g. TOE= (22/13.5) x (3.25-3.125)= 0.2 IN

STATIC CAMBER

The static camber is measured with the car at the correct hub and ride height by measuring the distance of a vertical string to a fixed surface (wheel or bump plate) mounted to the hub. There should be two measurements, one at the top of the surface, and the second at the bottom of the surface. The DIFFERENCE between these two readings TIMES 4 is the CAMBER in degrees if the plate is 14 inches high.

BUMP STEER CALCULATION

DIAL INDICATOR READINGS ARE (_____) INCHES APART

Height	Front of Plate	Minus	Rear of Plate	Equals	Difference
+3		-		=	
+2		-		=	
+1		-		=	
Zero	0.000	-	0.000	=	0.000
-1		-		=	
-2		-		=	
-3		-		=	

Wheel down relative to the frame is DROOP.
Wheel up relative to frame is BUMP.

Bump Steer Plate
and Dial Indicators

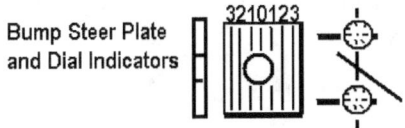

If the front indicator extends its pushrod inward faster than the rear indicator then the
wheel is toeing IN.

AT REAR:
TO REDUCE TOE IN ON BUMP SHORTEN THE TOP TRAILING ARM.
TO REDUCE TOE OUT ON BUMP LENGTHEN THE TOP TRAILING ARM.

AT FRONT:
(Assuming upward and outward slanting top link and tie-rod link, and assuming the tie-rod joint is spaced above the steering arm.)
ADDING SPACERS WILL REDUCE TOE OUT ON BUMP.
REMOVING SPACERS WILL REDUCE TOE IN ON BUMP.

43

VIII. REFERENCE

1. Jim Hall with David E. Davis Jr., "What Makes Cars Handle?", Ziff-Davis Publishing Co., Reprint from Car & Driver Magazine, Parts I & II.

2. Walter Bergman, Ford Motor Co., 1965, "The Basic Nature of Understeer-Oversteer".

3. Warren L. Harvey and D.B. Ressler Jr., "A Chassis Adjustment Analysis", P.M.E. Publications Box 191m Morristown, N.J. 07960.

4. Carroll Smith, "Prepare To Win - Part 6", Reprint from Sports Car Graphics, November 1970. pp 55-62.

5. Ron Wakefield, "Suspension & Handling", Road & Track Special Supplement, Reader Service Dept., Road & Track, 1499 Monrovia, Newport Beach, Ca. 92663.

IX. INDEX

Notes

Notes

www.ingramcontent.com/pod-product-compliance
Lightning Source LLC
Chambersburg PA
CBHW071258280526
45788CB00004B/1756